EMERGENCY MACHINES

CHRIS OXLADE

FIREFLY BOOKS

A FIREFLY BOOK

Published by Firefly Books Ltd. 2018
Copyright © 2017 Quarto Publishing plc

First printing

Publisher Cataloging-in-Publication Data (U.S.)

Library of Congress Control Number: 2018935564

Library and Archives Canada Cataloguing in Publication

Oxlade, Chris, author
        Emergency machines / Chris Oxlade.
ISBN 978-0-228-10112-3 (softcover)
        1. Emergency vehicles--Juvenile literature.
I. Title.
TL235.8.O95 2018   j629.222'34
C2018-901331-1

Published in the United States by
Firefly Books (U.S.) Inc.
P.O. Box 1338, Ellicott Station
Buffalo, New York 14205

Published in Canada by
Firefly Books Ltd.
50 Staples Avenue, Unit 1
Richmond Hill, Ontario L4B 0A7

Printed in Dongguan, China TL082018

Editor: Harriet Stone • Design: Dave Ball • Art Director: Malena Stojic • Editorial Director: Victoria Garrard

Acknowledgments
The publisher thanks the following agencies for their kind permission to use their images.

Key: bg = background, t = top, b = bottom, l = left, r = right, c = center

Alamy Stock Photo: back cover: Cultura Creative (RF); 2-3 © Paul Springett A; 5tl Cultura Creative (RF); 5r South West Images Scotland; 8-9bg Dembinsky Photo Associates; 9r ARMIN WEIGEL; 10t ABN IMAGES; 10b Olekcii Mach; 11c FORGET Patrick; 11b Andrew Harker; 12-13bg James Davies; 13br Robert McLean; 14-15bg Elizabeth Nunn; 15r FirePhoto; 17tr Stocktrek Images, Inc.; 17b Kevin Griffin; 18-19bg jason kay; 22-23bg Cameron Cormack; 24-25bg John Devlin; 25tl Mike Hesp; 28l Ashley Cooper; 28b CTK; 30-31bg Michael Routh; 34t Nick Fontana; 35tr REUTERS; 38-39bg mark unsworth; 39t David Osborn; 40b Chris Slack; 42-43bg dpa picture alliance archive; 43tl Marco McGinty; 43tr Cultura Creative (RF); 44-45bg EuroStyle Graphics; 46-47bg Agencja Fotograficzna Caro; 46b CPC Collection; **Dreamstime:** 6bg © Artzzz; 16t © Martingraf; 16b © Rico Leffanta; 19tl © Cvandyke; 19tr © Arenaphotouk; 19b © Mrdoomits; 33tr © Arenaphotouk; **istockPhoto:** 31cr ArrowImages **Shutterstock:** front cover: gary yim, meunierd; back cover: JASPERIMAGE, Christian Mueller, Tommy Alven; 1 Jaromir Chalabala; 4-5bg Ververidis Vasilis; 4tl Isaiah Shook; 4b VanderWolf Images; 5bl OgnjenO; 7tr Matthew Strauss; 7cl Andrew Harker; 7cr TFoxFoto; 7bl Mark Agnor; 7br Philip Bird LRPS CPAGB; 10-11bg Keith Muratori; 11t Tupungato; 13tl EML; 13tr deepspace; 13c george green; 13bl charl898; 16-17bg Phil MacD Photography; 17c FotograFFF; 19cl Steve Photography; 19cr MAC1; 20-21bg mikeledray; 21r blurAZ; 22t chippics; 22r Anton_Ivanov; 22b Art Konovalov; 23t 1000 Words; 23cr kay roxby; 23b TimBurgess; 25tr asharkyu; 25cl Brad Sauter; 25cr Belish; 25b wiktord; 26-27bg Lukasz Janyst; 26b Matt Ragen; 28-29bg efreet; 29t aragami12345s; 29cr msnobody; 29bl VanderWolf Images; 31tr Mark Agnor; 31cl supergenijalac; 31bl Kate_ryna; 31br John Huntington; 32-33bg supergenijalac; 34b Art Konovalov; 35c Gary Blakeley; 35br Gustavo Miguel Fernandes; 36-37bg charl898; 37t Leonard Zhukovsky; 37cl lidian Neeleman; 37cr ID1974; 37bl Newnow; 37br Ivan Cholakov; 40t Howard Pimborough; 41t avarand; 41c ID1974; 41b Cindy Haggerty; 43c Thanakrit Sathavornmanee; 43bl ANURAKE SINGTO-ON; 43br Africa Studio; 45t VanderWolf Images; 46t Pyty; 47tr Bychykhin Olexandr; 47c badahos; 47b ANURAKE SINGTO-ON

CONTENTS

EMERGENCY MACHINES

Welcome to the world of Emergency Machines! All the machines in this book help out when emergencies happen. They work in towns and cities, in the wilderness, on rivers and lakes, at airports, and out at sea. They help to search for missing people, rescue casualties, and put out raging fires.

What job do you think this tall machine would do?

Many emergency machines must be able to travel across rough, muddy, or snowy ground.

Every rescue mission needs special machines. As you read about each rescue job in this book, see if you can guess which machines would be used to get the job done!

Where do you think this rescue machine works?

Where would you be if this machine came to find you?

Ambulances, on the ground and in the air, transport casualties quickly to the hospital.

FIRE IN A BUILDING

When fire breaks out in a town or city building, firefighters rush to the scene in their fire-fighting machines. The machines carry the firefighters themselves, plenty of water, and all the equipment the firefighters will need to tackle a fire.

Which machines would you choose?

Pumper

Hydraulic platform

Fire-bombing plane

Drone

Inshore lifeboat

FIRE TRUCK

The proper name for this type of fire truck is "turntable ladder." It has a ladder that reaches high into the air. Firefighters climb the ladder to spray water high up on burning buildings and to rescue trapped people from windows and roofs.

The turntable lets the ladder swing from side to side.

The driver and other firefighters travel in the cab.

Outriggers are legs that stop the truck from toppling over when the ladder is up.

The sections of the ladder slide out to make it longer.

At the top of the ladder there is a platform for firefighters and a nozzle to spray water.

A water pump pushes water through hoses to be sprayed onto the fire.

TURNTABLE LADDER IN NUMBERS

LENGTH: 49 feet

LADDER LENGTH: 164 feet

TOP SPEED: 62 miles per hour

CITY FIRE MACHINES

Here are all the different machines that help to fight city fires.

1 MOBILE COMMAND UNIT

A mobile command unit is a mobile base where fire chiefs or leading firefighters plan how to fight a fire. It has video cameras on tall towers and communication equipment inside.

2 DRONE

Firefighters send a drone up to work as eyes in the sky above a fire. Video from a drone shows the firefighters where flames are burning.

3 PUMPER

Firefighters connect long hoses to the pump on a general-purpose pumper. The pump sucks water from a fire hydrant and pushes it along the hoses.

4 TURNTABLE LADDER

A turntable ladder arrives to help rescue people from tall buildings, or to spray water into windows from its long ladder.

5 HYDRAULIC PLATFORM

A hydraulic platform has a long, jointed arm with a platform at the end. The arm reaches over roofs to let firefighters spray water down onto a fire.

WATER RESCUE

Lakes, rivers, and coasts can be dangerous places. People sometimes get into trouble when they are swimming or boating, or when they fall into the water accidentally. Floods are an added danger. Rescuers use boats and other special machines to rescue people from water.

Which of these machines would rescuers need for a water rescue?

?

Inflatable boat

?

Fire boat

?

Airport fire truck

?

Offshore lifeboat

?

Amphibious tracked vehicle

RESCUE HOVERCRAFT

A hovercraft is a machine that's half boat, half aircraft. It rides on a cushion of air, skimming over land or water. This makes it a very useful machine for emergency rescues on muddy riverbanks, shallow water, and even in quicksand!

Air from fans is directed from side to side by rudders, which make the hovercraft turn left or right.

An engine powers the fans that blow air into the skirt, and the fans that push the hovercraft along.

The main fan blows air into the space under the hovercraft, making its cushion of air.

The driver sits at the front, controlling the hovercraft with a steering wheel and levers.

Propulsion fans work like aircraft propellers. They push the hovercraft along.

A rubber skirt around the base of the hovercraft holds the cushion of air in place.

RESCUE HOVERCRAFT IN NUMBERS

LENGTH: 26 feet

TOP SPEED: 34 miles per hour

WEIGHT: 4.4 tons

CREW: 2 to 4

WATER RESCUE MACHINES

Here are all the emergency machines that help to rescue people in water.

① INFLATABLE BOAT

A tough inflatable boat is perfect for rescuing people in trouble. It can be taken to where it's needed on a road trailer and launched quickly into the water. It's driven along by an engine with a propeller, called an outboard motor.

② JET SKI

Beach lifeguards often have a jet ski ready and waiting in case anybody gets into trouble in the sea close to the beach. A jet ski skims across the water to reach a casualty quickly.

AMPHIBIOUS VEHICLE

This machine can drive across land or move through water. It comes into action if people are stuck in places where boats can't get to easily, such as very shallow water, deep mud, or water with broken ice on top.

4 RESCUE HOVERCRAFT

Here's another machine that's used when people are stuck in shallow water, mud, or ice. It skims across land and water on a cushion of air.

5 FIRE BOAT

If there's a fire on the banks of a river, or on a boat or ship, a fire boat comes to the rescue. It's like a floating fire truck.

ROAD ACCIDENT

A road accident happens when a vehicle slides off a road or bumps into another vehicle. Road accidents are caused by wet or icy roads, or by drivers making mistakes. Emergency vehicles come to the rescue of casualties and help to clear the road.

Which machines would you choose?

?

Police motorcycle

?

Water bomber

?

Off-road rescue vehicle

?

Air ambulance

?

Ambulance

AMBULANCE

An ambulance is a medical emergency vehicle. On board are expert paramedics and all the equipment they need to treat casualties. The casualties are loaded into an ambulance on stretchers to take them to the hospital.

There is medical equipment stored on the walls and in cabinets. The equipment includes a defibrillator for restarting a patient's heart and oxygen tanks.

AMBULANCE IN NUMBERS

LENGTH: 20 feet

TOP SPEED: 96 miles per hour

ENGINE SIZE: 0.7 gallons

CREW: 2 paramedics

There are seats for the paramedics and for casualties with minor injuries.

Flashing lights and sirens warn other road users that an ambulance is coming and it's in a hurry.

Paramedics travel in the cab. Here there's a radio for them to keep in touch with their base and satellite navigation to guide them to the scene of an accident.

The stretcher rolls on wheels and turns into a bed inside the ambulance.

ROAD ACCIDENT MACHINES

Here are all the machines that help at a road accident.

1 POLICE MOTORCYCLE

A police motorcycle is large, powerful, and fast. It is normally the first machine to arrive at the scene of an accident. The police rider reports back on the accident and calls other emergency services to the scene.

2 POLICE CAR

A police car is next to arrive at the scene. Its lights and sirens warn other road users that there's an accident ahead. The car carries useful equipment, such as cones for blocking off the road, and a first-aid kit.

3 RESCUE TRUCK

Vehicles that are damaged in accidents can't be driven away. So a rescue truck comes along to pick them up and carry them to be fixed or scrapped.

4 AMBULANCE

If anybody is seriously injured, the police call for an ambulance. When the ambulance arrives, paramedics jump out and decide which casualties need treatment. The ambulance carries the casualties to the hospital.

5 FIRE TRUCK

A fire truck comes to the scene if a driver or passenger is trapped inside a vehicle. The truck carries special cutting equipment to rip off car doors or slice off car roofs.

6 AIR AMBULANCE

Occasionally a casualty needs to get to the hospital very quickly. Then a special helicopter called an air ambulance is called. It has all the equipment that a normal ambulance carries and can fly to a nearby hospital in a few minutes.

WILDERNESS RESCUE

Walkers, climbers, and tourists sometimes have accidents or get lost in the wilderness. Rescuers use machines which can travel over rough terrain and snow. Helicopters are used to search from the air.

Which of these machines would rescuers need for a wilderness rescue?

?

4x4 truck

?

Bulldozer

?

Police car

?

Snowmobile

?

Rescue helicopter

RESCUE HELICOPTER

Rescuers get a good view of the ground from a helicopter, so this machine is useful for searching for casualties. A helicopter can land in a small space to pick up those in need, or hover above them while crew members descend to the ground.

The main rotor lifts the helicopter into the air. It is made up of a central hub and long rotor blades.

The pilots sit in the cockpit with a radio, navigation equipment, and a thermal-imaging camera to spot casualties in the dark.

RESCUE HELICOPTER IN NUMBERS

LENGTH: 46.6 feet

ROTOR SIZE: 51.5 feet

ENGINES: 2 x turboshaft

TOP SPEED: 160 miles per hour

The winch lowers crew members to the ground on a strong wire and lifts casualties back up.

The spinning tail rotor controls how the helicopter turns left and right.

There is first-aid equipment and stretchers for casualties in the main cabin.

The winch is worked by an electric motor. A crewmember wears a body harness when being lowered and lifted.

WILDERNESS RESCUE MACHINES

Here are all the emergency machines that help to rescue people in the wilderness.

1 OFF-ROAD RESCUE TRUCK

Rescuers travel as far as they can into the wilderness in off-road trucks. Rescue equipment is carried inside and on the roof of the truck. The trucks also carry casualties to safety.

2 QUAD BIKE

A quad bike is like a motorcycle with four wheels instead of two. This quad bike has tracks instead of wheels for working on snow. It can tow a stretcher trailer.

3 RESCUE HELICOPTER

Rescuers on the ground sometimes call in a rescue helicopter to help with a search, or to pick up sick or injured casualties and transport them to the hospital.

4 SNOWMOBILE

A snowmobile has skids at the front and a track at the rear that drives it along. Rescuers use snowmobiles for search and rescue in winter when there's snow on the ground.

5 SKI RESCUE VEHICLE

This vehicle is normally used to smooth over ski slopes, but it's also used to rescue injured skiers. Its wide tracks grip the ground, even on steep slopes.

FIRE IN THE FOREST

Forest fires rage when trees, shrubs, and dry twigs and branches catch fire. They are also called bushfires or wildfires. Lightning strikes—and more often careless campers or tourists—set off forest fires. Special machines are needed to fight these fires, as there are few roads and the landscape is often hilly.

Which of these machines would you need to fight a forest fire?

Off-road fire truck

Water bomber

Bulldozer

Turntable ladder

Fireboat

WATER BOMBER

The easiest way to tackle a forest fire is to drop water on it from the sky. This is the job of a water bomber—an aircraft with a big water tank inside. The bomber collects water from a lake or river and dumps it onto the flames. This water bomber is a Bombardier CL-415.

The water tank is inside the plane's fuselage. A trapdoor opens to let the water out.

WATER BOMBER IN NUMBERS

LENGTH: 65 feet

WINGSPAN: 94 feet

TOP SPEED: 224 miles per hour

WATER CAPACITY: 6.7 tons

The water bomber skims across the sea, scooping water into its tank.

Two pilots fly the bomber from the cockpit. It takes a lot of skill to fly a water bomber.

This water bomber has two turboprop engines.

Undercarriage wheels fold down so the water bomber can land on a runway.

The boat-shaped hull is needed for taking off from and landing on water.

FOREST FIRE MACHINES

Here are all the emergency machines that help to fight forest fires.

1 4X4 FIRE TRUCK

When somebody reports that a forest fire has started, a small 4x4 fire truck is sent to investigate. The truck carries equipment to tackle small fires.

2 OFF-ROAD FIRE TRUCK

A bigger truck is needed for more ferocious fires. This tough emergency machine has big wheels for going over rough ground, an on-board water tank, pumps, and hoses.

BULLDOZER

Firefighters use bulldozers to clear gaps in the forest. The gaps are called firebreaks and they are designed to stop a fire from spreading. The bulldozer knocks down trees and clears undergrowth.

4 WATER BOMBER

If fire trucks can't reach a fire, or a fire is too big for them to tackle, firefighters call in a water bomber. The bomber drops water onto the flames. Pilots can report to firefighters how a fire is spreading.

5 FIRE HELICOPTER

A fire helicopter does the same job as a water bomber, but it can't carry as much water. The helicopter scoops up water in a fabric bucket dangling on a wire. Firefighters also travel in helicopters.

SEA RESCUE

When boats, ships, and sometimes planes get into trouble far out at sea, a special set of emergency machines comes to the rescue. They often battle strong winds and monstrous waves as they search for missing sailors and pull them to safety.

Which of these machines would you use in a sea rescue?

Police motorcycle

Coastguard helicopter

Patrol boat

Drone

Long-range spotter plane

OFFSHORE LIFEBOAT

Rescuers need a tough rescue boat when they venture out to sea. An offshore lifeboat does the job. It's very strong, very fast, and handles all but the very worst winds and waves with ease. It's also self-righting, which means if a wave knocks it over, it pops back up again.

Radar shows where other boats and ships are. There's also an aerial for the radio, which the crew uses to keep in touch with other rescue vessels and aircraft.

OFFSHORE LIFEBOAT IN NuMBERS

LENGTH: 56.8 feet

WEIGHT: 46.3 tons

ENGINE: 2 x diesel engines

TOP SPEED: 25 knots

CREW: 7

There is space for casualties in a cabin below the watertight wheelhouse, complete with stretchers and medical equipment.

The crew can operate the boat from the flying bridge, which gives them a good view of the sea around the boat.

Lifeboats carry smaller inflatable dinghies that are used when rescuers need to venture into shallow water close to the shore.

The guard rail keeps the crew safe as they move around on deck in bumpy seas.

The boat has a very strong hull with a sharp bow that cuts easily through the waves.

SEA RESCUE MACHINES

Here are all the emergency machines that help to rescue people in trouble at sea.

1 INSHORE LIFEBOAT

An inshore lifeboat deals with emergencies around the coast. It has a solid hull with a tough inflatable tube around the edge, and powerful outboard motors.

2 OFFSHORE LIFEBOAT

If a boat or ship is too far out to sea for an inshore lifeboat to reach it, an offshore lifeboat is launched instead. As well as picking up casualties, it can also tow boats back to land.

③ RESCUE HELICOPTER

A rescue helicopter joins in with a rescue to help search for missing boats or ships, or spot people in the water. It also picks up injured casualties and carries them to the hospital on shore.

④ PATROL SHIP

A patrol ship carries out search and rescue missions far out into the ocean, where offshore lifeboats and helicopters can't reach.

⑤ PATROL PLANE

A patrol plane is called out to search huge areas of ocean for missing boats and ships. It can drop supplies to casualties and then guide a patrol ship to the right location.

AIRPORT RESCUE

Airport emergency machines are always on standby when planes are taking off and landing. Their crews are ready to leap into action if a plane has to make an emergency landing. These machines are specially designed for keeping airfields safe and for putting out fires on planes.

Which machines would you need for an airport emergency?

?

Airport Response vehicle

?

Fire truck with stinger

?

Snowmobile

?

Robot fire fighter

?

Rescue truck

AIRPORT FIRE TRUCK

There's always a risk of fire when a plane makes an emergency landing. An airport fire truck is there to put out fires, and firefighters also help passengers and crew to safety. An airport fire truck sprays foam onto burning fuel, which smothers the flames.

Inside the fire truck is a big tank full of water. The water is mixed with chemicals to make foam that is then sprayed onto the fire.

This vehicle is built to travel across rough, muddy airfields. It has eight wheels with chunky tires.

Equipment is stored in these lockers.

Flashing lights and sirens make the fire truck easy to see and hear.

An airport fire truck's main weapon is this nozzle, also called a monitor. It shoots foam at a fire. The crew aims it from the cab.

An onboard pump pushes foam out of the tank and through the nozzle.

The crew operate the truck while sitting inside the cab.

AIRPORT FIRE TRUCK IN NUMBERS

LENGTH: 39 feet

TOP SPEED: 84 miles per hour

WATER TANK CAPACITY: 3,300 gallons

MAXIMUM WEIGHT: 57.3 tons

AIRPORT RESCUE MACHINES

Here are all the emergency machines that help to rescue people in trouble at an airport.

1 BIRD-SCARING TRUCK

Some accidents are caused by aircraft hitting birds as they take off. So most airports have vehicles that drive around the airfield using loud noise to scare away large flocks of birds.

2 RESPONSE VEHICLE

A fast-response truck races across the airfield to reach the scene of an emergency. The crew on board can call in other emergency vehicles, such as fire trucks.

3 FIRE TRUCK

An airport fire truck is called into action if there is ever a chance of a fire breaking out on an aircraft. It covers the aircraft in foam, which smothers any flames.

4 STINGER

This fire truck is armed with a special device called a stinger, on the end of an arm. The stinger pierces through an aircraft's metal fuselage and sprays water or foam inside.

5 ROBOT FIRE FIGHTER

Robot airport fire-fighting machines are being tested. A robot can approach a hot fire on its tracks, where it would be too dangerous for human firefighters to go.

ANSWERS

Fire in a building (page 7)

✓ Hydraulic platform

✓ Pumper

✓ Drone

Water rescue (page 13)

✓ Inflatable boat

✓ Amphibious tracked vehicle

✓ Fire boat

Road accident (page 19)

✓ Police motorcycle

✓ Ambulance

✓ Air ambulance

Wilderness rescue (page 25)

✓ 4x4 truck

✓ Rescue helicopter

✓ Snowmobile

Fire in the forest (page 31)

✓ Water bomber

✓ Off-road fire truck

✓ Bulldozer

Sea rescue (page 37)

✓ Coastguard helicopter

✓ Patrol boat

✓ Long-range spotter plane

Airport rescue (page 43)

✓ Airport Response vehicle

✓ Fire truck with stinger

✓ Robot fire fighter